Pieces in the Form of a Pear

William Minor

Black Centipede Press
Denver, CO
blackcentipedepress@gmail.com

ISBN #: 978-1-7353275-3-2

Design, Layout, Edit: Ivan Do
Cover Art: Ivan Do

for Linda

The poet is a repeater.

-Alejandro Zambra

Briefly I considered Paris.
I considered it as a place for birds
and then I considered it as a place
for buildings.

Even though
women look alike
they may be
distinguished easily.

In sacred cultures
the head was an object
of tremendous significance,
but in normal cultures
it was just a head.

Ron Silliman

Ron Silliman, emerging from behind
the armoire, just hours after leaving
the door open and letting the mosquitoes in,
moments before leaning against the refrigerator
and waiting for the water to boil.

Animals can stand outside for hours.

Situations

Situations are reasonable. I like drinks
and sausages. I like drinks and then sausages
and then I like sausages and then drinks.
The most elementary form of liking is liking
drinks and then sausages and then sausages
and then drinks.

Language can be very exciting
when a woman you're interested in
tells you something you were hoping
to hear about yourself.

Japan

I have never been to Japan,
but I'm sure they're doing their best
over there.

Woman

Rolling off the bench towards us
was the supple figure of the woman
who greeted us in the courtyard,
the one who spoke of her childhood
interest in science.

Two Figures

It is normal to have
a story to tell,
and it is normal to have
to listen to a man
tell a story sometimes.

Nicolas Chamfort

Sometimes your butler finds you
on the floor in a pool of blood
after you've lost your nose
and failed to apply a paper cutter
to your neck properly.

False World

A false sense of the world
is perfectly acceptable
in cases where a false world
is all that presents itself.

Landscape

Sometimes when surroundings change
a little more wood appears,
and sometimes this increase in wood
leads to an irritating change in feeling.

Picasso

Picasso opened one of the cabinets. The pots
and pans were perfectly in place. Later, he sat
in a wooden armchair and said some things about
the Spanish military. In the evening, he paired
a Catalan peasant with a couple of pigeons. Eventually,
he moved into the dining room, where he found an
old banana turning brown on a laminated table.

Rooster

Of course
a rooster sounds
interesting.

The Goal Today

The goal today is to write
something long about something
important, or, at the very least,
something short about something
meaningless, or something of average
length about something typical.

Self-Portrait

I sometimes wonder
if I will ever see
a beautiful Spanish woman
completely naked.

Seated Man

The oddest use
for a seated man
is thought.

There can be no mistaking
the tone of a person
who speaks of women
in an average way.

Khlebnikov and Kharms

Khlebnikov looked at Kharms, Kharms looked at Khlebnikov. Khlebnikov knew it was stupid to be looking at Kharms, Kharms knew it was stupid to be looking at Khlebnikov. It was a stupid situation, and Khlebnikov knew it was a situation, and Kharms knew it was a situation.

The back of a woman's head is just hair.

Monkey

The days are filled with
this feeling of being a monkey,
of being at this moment
this tiresome little monkey.

Some Women

Some women are good but not interesting.
Some women are interesting but not good.
Some women are neither good nor interesting.
Some women are very good and very interesting.
Some women are very good but not very interesting.
Some women are very interesting but not very good.

The Philosopher

A thoughtful man
can leap into a crater
if he wants to.

Jean-Pierre

Jean-Pierre took on
a somber cast
when he appeared
in the more poetic form
of waiting for her to finish
her sentence on him.

A Horse

A horse may also have
a tragic system of thought
that revolves primarily around
horses.

Two Men

Sometimes a man writes a book
that isn't very exciting,
and one day a man says to him
aren't you the man who wrote that book
that wasn't very exciting.

Courbet

In his later years,
Courbet divided his time
between small talk
and visiting people.

Sitting alone
in the room
with an erection,
how stupid.

How does
one investigate
the conditions
in which a woman
might appear.

Germany

Germany is very German.
Extremely German, even.
Too German? It's hard to say.
It just seems very German.

Writing

Instead of writing about something crucial and serious,
something heartfelt and necessary,
you end up thinking about something absurd and
mundane, something you wish you had written.

Turn aside, see less horse. See less horse, see less horse.

Mexico

Mexico is a big place
with lots of mountains and
all kinds of things to say
to people I said to a woman.

Charles Olson

I’m glad I’m not
the kind of poet who likes
to sit around all night
talking about Charles Olson.

Landscape

Dogs are small and active.
Women are larger and more stationary.

A List of Lizards

The Mexican Beaded Lizard
The Tokay Gecko
The Collared Lizard
The Jesus Lizard
The Basilisk

Braque

Braque would often
walk into a room
and ask his wife what
was good in there.

Los Angeles

Sometimes a woman appears
in very little clothing
on a billboard high above a building
with a taco on it. It is of no use
to want to fuck a woman like that

Sergei Esenin

It must have been
very difficult to have
been Sergei Esenin
there towards the end.

Self-Portrait

The events
of daily life
often remind me
of the dreams
I used to have.

Mallarmé

When I look at a beautiful woman
I don't think of Mallarmé,
but when I look at a regular woman
I sometimes think of Rimbaud.

Girl

A strange man
sits on a strange horse
and a strange dog looks at him.
I understand how empty
it makes her feel.

The Frenchman

It is easy to imagine a Frenchman
making too much
of a woman enjoying herself.

The Leg

In certain situations,
a woman's leg
acts as a dazzling catalyst
for the transformation of all things.
In others, it's just a leg

Images

Images that are
suitable for children
include pine trees
and a man at night.

Dog

It is possible
for a lost dog
to look and act
like a regular dog.

Rousseau

I like to think of Rousseau
as caught in a web of palmettoes,
taking a long, revitalizing look
at the beautiful woman on the sofa
just before he is swallowed whole
by the jaws of an imaginary lion.

There are certain
exaggerated conditions
which make being
a genuine possibility.

Even vegetarians
run the risk
of eating Pythagoras.

Man at a Table

It is a sacred thing
to look at a man sitting at a table,
provided you are no longer
a man yourself, and he isn't trying
to tell you a story.

The Conversation

If we are going to talk about meaning,
we are going to have to talk about
the women who have lost their meaning,
but everybody knows it's no fun to talk about
a woman who has lost her meaning.

Gentleness
in extreme form
can be realistic.

Madeleine Bernard

Imagine what
Madeleine Bernard
would look like
sitting in a cottage.

Landscape

It's true we're out here
killing each other,
but it's also true we're out here
looking at each other.

The Bystander

A lot of the women here like
to walk around the property
and expose their beauty in a way
that suits them, but doesn't overwhelm
the virtue of the average bystander.

The Horses

It's up to the horses
to develop a debilitating awareness
of horse death.

Imagine
the kind of poet
it would take
to want to add variety
to his work.

Landscape

Inner meaning is fine,
but it can lead to the falsification
of other types of meaning,
the kind that occur in most landscapes,
for example.

Llama

If a llama spits on you,
his case has been made.

Mortality

Mortality has
a way of reminding
some French women
what their lives are like
in certain poems.

Self-Portrait

I had the creamy tomato bisque,
the thin crust margherita pizza,
and a nine ounce glass of pinot noir
from the Willamette Valley.

It is easy to shrug off
the essential points
of Roman philosophy.

Picasso

Picasso was right –
suffering over
a pale young woman
who isn't around
is a perfect occupation
for a poet.

It is true
I know more
than you do
of the tribulations
of courtly love.

Hegel's Holiday

The easiest way
for a philosopher
to lose his meaning
is to lose it in the mind
of another man.

The Conversation

She said something, but I didn't understand it.
Then I said something, but she didn't understand it.
She repeated what she said, but I still didn't understand it,
so I repeated what she said, but then she didn't understand it.
So we both just stood there.

Saint Augustine

As Saint Augustine said:
I know what she is when
they don't ask me, but when
they ask me, I don't know.

Peru

People move to Peru
to fuck and eat
whatever they have down in Peru.

Apollinaire

It is easy to imagine
what Apollinaire's thoughts
looked like, but Picasso claimed
that the inside of Apollinaire's body
was ridiculous.

Imagine
the kind of man
it would take
to refer to a work of art
as unconvincing.

The Dog

I hate what happened
to the dog, but again,
it wasn't even our dog.

André Breton

I like it when
André Breton
compares his
lover's tongue to
a stabbed wafer.

The Thinker

Gratuitous contemplation
has delivered me into
a kind of imaginary stupidity.

Self-Portrait

I wouldn't want her
to see me with my intestines
out on the table, even if
they're just being cleaned.

The Vision

A profound revelation
on the deepest nature
of love, beauty and the self
may turn out to be nothing more
than a simple visual mishap.

Rabbit

Sometimes a rabbit is interesting
because a man talks about it
with enthusiasm, and sometimes it is
the rabbit itself that is interesting.

There are
a lot of ways
to express
what it feels like
to be a girl.

The Mountain

If a man should ask to meet me
at the summit of a mountain
to discuss the great questions of life,
I would have to turn him down

Some Men

Some men passionately support
the town's antiquated heating system.

Two Figures

I nearly stood up.
She nearly spoke to me.
I nearly responded.
She went the other way.
I nearly followed her.

Magritte

No Magritte at one table,
no Magritte at another table.
All signs point to an absence
of Magritte at two tables.

Talking Woman

A woman with a coarse voice
can be very sexy,
especially if she only says
the most negative things.

It is difficult
to speak of
the ideal women
without speaking of
the regular ones.

John Dryden

I have nothing to say about John Dryden.
John Dryden is not the point here.
The only thing I will say about John Dryden
is that he lost the battle with appearances.

Recurring bouts of unease
often lead to recurring bouts
of interest in it.

Woman

Looking at a woman wasn't very funny back then.
It's not very funny now, either.
In fact, I can't remember the last time I looked at a woman
and thought it was funny.

Self-Portrait

I like the
big machines
that men ride
in warehouses.

Bordeaux

Bordeaux is a great town for asking
a woman what she thinks of it,
and it is a great town for her telling you
she thinks it is pleasant enough.

Men

Men have ideas
that some consider good ones,
but it isn't true.

Woman Walking

Solitude is tough
and the Christ is rotten,
says the walking woman
on a mild afternoon.

Table

In keeping with the general practice
of looking at things
and then saying something about them,
Paolo looked over at the table and said,
"I don't like it."

Women

One of the things
I like about women
is that they will punch a bear
repeatedly in the face
and then throw rocks at it.

Jean Henri Fabre and the Dung Beetle

By observing the behavior of the beetle very closely,
he was able to determine that it was interested in shit,
and that if it gathered enough shit, other beetles might
also develop an interest in shit, and then try to steal it.

The Vegetable Seller

The vegetable seller
wore a brown blouse
with yellow buttons on it.

The Conversation

Did you ever find the pears?
No.

Horses

The horses look like good spirits.
They do not deny their religious impulses,
and they do not engage in useless experiments
intended to prove that they are horses.

Language

I like language,
but I don't really care
what happens to it.